There's a green light all around me
There's a green light fills the skies
There's a green light that surrounds me
and it's looking in my eyes . . .

Rhinestone Rhino
and Other Poems

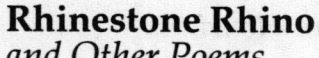

[handwritten dedication] tor
Tom, Sam
+ Victoria
love

[handwritten signature] Adrian
Henri

Also by Adrian Henri

Box and Other Poems
The Phantom Lollipop Lady and Other Poems
Eric the Punk Cat

ADRIAN HENRI
Rhinestone Rhino
and Other Poems

ILLUSTRATED BY TONY ROSS

MAMMOTH

To Nina, Nell, Antoinette and Marie.

First published in Great Britain 1989
by Methuen Children's Books Ltd
Published 1991 by Mammoth
an imprint of Mandarin Paperbacks
Michelin House, 81 Fulham Road, London SW3 6RB

Mandarin is an imprint of the Octopus Publishing Group

Text copyright © 1989 Adrian Henri
Illustrations copyright © 1989 Tony Ross

ISBN 0 7497 0111 0

A CIP catalogue record for this title
is available from the British Library

Printed in Great Britain
by Cox and Wyman Ltd, Reading, Berkshire

Contents

Rhinestone Rhino   7

Kate   10

Menu   12

Adios Amigos   15

Paracetamol   17

Black Marks   19

Rover   20

Oh Dear   23

City Hedges   24

A Question of Colour   27

In a Field   28

Nevermore   30

Gordon Bennett   32

Twin Poem No. 1   35

Twin Poem No. 2   36

The Heart Poem   37

Poets   40

Autumn Haiku   42

Haiku: City Park in Winter   43

Wartime Child   44

The Dark   54

Shazia   56

Pedestrian   58

On Taking a Walk in the
    Pleasant Countryside   59

Fashion   60

Crowfield   62

Goalposts   65

The Green Light   66

Mr McManus   68

Ideal Gnome   70

Rhinestone Rhino

Ah'm a rhinestone rhino
From the lone star state
Ah'm a Country n' Western
All time great

Ah'm a ten-ton Texas
Bunch o'joy
Ah'm a rhin-o-ceros
Good ol' boy

Ah'm a rhinestone rhino –
ceros yodel-ay-ee

At the Grand Old Opry
Ah'm a superstar
When ah sings ma songs
And strums ma guit-ar

Ah began ma life
In a country shack
Now ah rides around
In a Cad-ill-ac

Ah'm a rhinestone rhino –
ceros yodel-ay-ee

There's Tammy n' Dolly n'
Emmy Lou
And Johnny Cash is King
It's true

But the pride of Gnashville,
Tennessee
Is your five-by-five star
Lil' ol' me

Ah'm a rhinestone rhino –
ceros yodel-ay-ee

Ah'm a rhine –
  stone
    rhino –

      ceros
      yodel
        ay –
          eeee

Kate

I think I'm in love with Kate
it can't just be her dimples
it's not as simple
as that.

Shirley's blonde and Sue's hair's red
and curly. But I like dark hair
short and straight
like Kate.

I think that I'm too late.
She'll go straight home. Perhaps
she'll wait and say
'Hello'.

I'll walk home past her street.
Perhaps I'll meet her on the way.
I won't know what
to say.

I pulled her hair and called her names today
She ran away. I'm *sure* she knows
that I'm in love
with Kate.

Menu

Breakfasting off kedgeree,
though rather grand,
is not quite the thing for me.
In Barcelona, on the other hand,
Catalan Spinach sounds just right
after a night on the Ramblas.
I can handle a haggis anytime,
though Burns Night's best.
As for the rest, I could be
in Normandy, eating goose,
and carbonnade's a good excuse
for buying beer. Meanwhile, back here,
there's only eggs to scramble
(not very thrilling)

or some liquorice allsorts
(not very filling); and

the shops are closed (sad
to say), so I suppose
it's a Chinese takeaway.

Adios Amigos . . .

¡THE MEXICANS ARE COMING!
The whisper goes round the school
persistent as the smell of garlic.
Strange sounds come from the kitchens,
Mariachi Bands and maraccas,
Shouts of 'Olé'. They're going crackers.

¡THE MEXICANS ARE HERE!
Rumour spreads, hot as chili-powder.
The dinner-ladies burst through the kitchen door
clapping their hands, stamping their heels on the floor.
Brightly-coloured shawls swirl. Boys and girls
watch, wide-eyed as a bullfight crowd.

¡THE MEXICANS HAVE COME!
Michelle's mum serves Tropical Dessert
with a flick of her skirt. Her friends serve
Chile con Chips, Baked Beans y Tortillas
wearing black lace mantillas. It tastes
really nice, and it's just the same price.

¡THE MEXICANS HAVE BEEN!
They haven't been seen for days. Just aprons of green
and the clatter of trays. Distant as holidays
and a tropical moon. I hope they come back soon.
The Headmaster's put his sombrero away.
'Cos nothing's the same since that wonderful day
when we all cried 'Olé',
    when the Mexicans came . . .

Paracetamol

for Spike Sterne

If a giraffe has a headache
Or a chimpanzee has a fall
There's no aspirins in the jungle
'Cause the parrots ate 'em all.

Black Marks

Why does he leave paw-marks
all over the sink? You'd think
he'd learn to wipe his paws:
I'll bet yours does, politely.
He wakes me up twice nightly,
sitting on my chest. The rest
of the time he sleeps on top of
anything you might want,
or stands between you and the T.V.,
so you can't see. Now
he's walked all over
this nice clean page: no wonder
he gets me in a rage.
Why is he always out
when you want him in?
Or in when you want him out?
He's the worst cat in the world,
no doubt about it, but he's the
only one we've got. I suppose
I'd miss him quite a lot . . .
I wonder if he'd miss me?
Ow, get your claws out!
. . . see?

Rover

for David Ross

I have a pet oyster called Rover.
He lives in the bathroom sink
and is never any trouble:
no birdseed or tins of Kennomeat,
no cat-litter.
We don't need to take him for walks,
we don't need an oyster-flap in the back door.

He doesn't bark
or sing,
just lies in the sink
and never says a thing.
Sometimes,
when he feels irritable,
he grits his teeth
and produces a little pearl.

At night,
we tuck him up snug in his oyster-bed
until the bathroom tide comes in
in the morning.

Sometimes
I look at Rover and say
'The world's your lobster,
Rover', I say.

Oh Dear

Someone's let the cat out of the bag
And put it amongst the pigeons.

City Hedges

There are pinstripe hedges
Trees wear bowler hats
Bushes like umbrellas
All the cows wear spats

Fish commute downriver
Rush to catch the tide
Birds clock in at daybreak
Lunchbox by their side

The banks are full of blackberries
With walls of thistledown
The sheep are in the typing-pool:

The country's come to town!

A Question of Colour

for Tony Griffiths

Everyone knows
a chameleon changes colour from its toes
upwards.
What if two of them met
toe to toe,
with not enough room to go
forward or back,
in a plain grey space.
Which would lose face?
Would one turn white
and the other black?
Or would the two
slowly disappear from view?
I can't work it out.
Can you?

In a Field

Here's two more of them:
the funny ones with only two legs,
no horns,
and hardly any hair.

Yes, little ones this time
I'll go and have a closer look.

I know,
Let's follow them. For fun.

Look!
They've started to run . . .

Nevermore

The cat is turning into a crow.
This morning it sprouted feathers,
now it's grown a wing.
There isn't a thing we can do
about it. Now its paws
have started to go.
I'm *sure* it's turning into a crow;
it used to sit and say 'miaow'
before: now it stands on one leg
and goes 'caw'.

It perched all last night on top of the telly,
saying 'NEVERMORE'.
There it is again, flapping its wings
at the cat-flap in the back door.
It *has* turned into a crow, it's true:
it's just flown off down the Avenue.

Gordon Bennett

Gordon Bennett's always there
In the kitchen, on the stairs,
Never leaves your socks in pairs
Gordon Bennett doesn't care!

Gordon's name's on everybody's lips:
If they drop a bag of fish-and-chips,
Or break a plate, or their train's late,
Or someone's left a rollerskate
Just where they put their foot,
Without a doubt
'*Gordon Bennett!*' They cry out.

Gordon Bennett doesn't care
In the classroom, at the sink,
'My team's lost!' 'I've spilt my drink.'
Gordon Bennett's always there!

Gordon always seems to get the blame
Everywhere you'll hear them call his name:
'*Gordon Bennett*! Where's that cat?'
'*Gordon Bennett*! Who left that
Just where I'd fall over it?'
In snow or rain
'*Gordon Bennett*'s' the refrain.

Gordon Bennett's always there
In the kitchen, on the stairs,
Never leaves your socks in pairs
Gordon Bennett doesn't care!

Twin Poem No. 1

Don't worry
if you see another poem
looking exactly like
me:
really we're words apart
and only look alike
until you see us
together.

Twin Poem No. 2

Don't worry
if you see another
poem
looking exactly like me:
really we're words
apart
and only look
alike
until you see us together.

The Heart Poem

(for three voices)
for Jackie, Karen and Glynn,
Stirchley Upper School,
and The British Heart Foundation

the hands of the clock move
minute
by minute   by minute   by minute

the digits shift
second
by second   by second   by second

arteries slow
minute
by minute   by minute   by minute

veins stiffen
second
by second   by second   by second

the last tube-train
pulls into the platform
minute
by minute   by minute   by minute

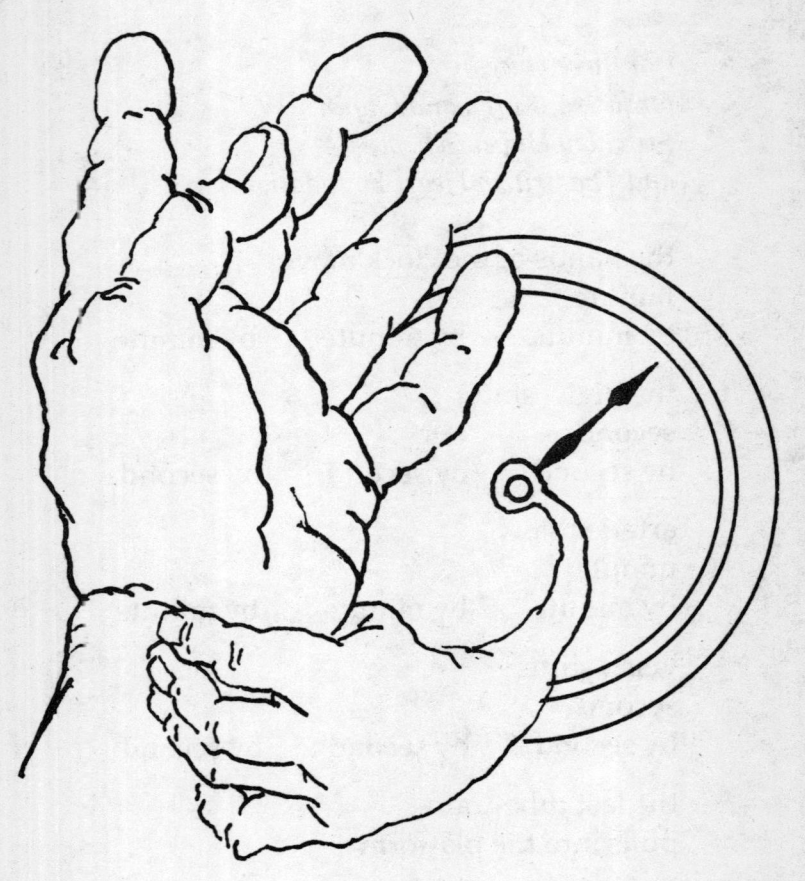

a barge clogged with weeds
on the silted canal
second
by second   by second   by second

the line on the graph paper
slowly straightens
minute
by minute   by minute   by minute

the small green dot on the screen
slowly fading
second
by second   by second   by second

one last
minute   minute   minute
one last
second   second   second
before
the
silence   silence   silence

Poets

can't compete
with clowns.
When they try to juggle words
they trip over nouns,
drop their 'h's'
trap their verbs between the pages,
try to pull rhymes out of a hat,
adjectives that just fall flat;
sentences that fail to start,
paragraphs that come apart.

Clowns can tumble,
clowns can fumble,
clowns can laugh
and clowns can grumble.

Everybody
loves a clown:
no one laughs
when the poet falls down.

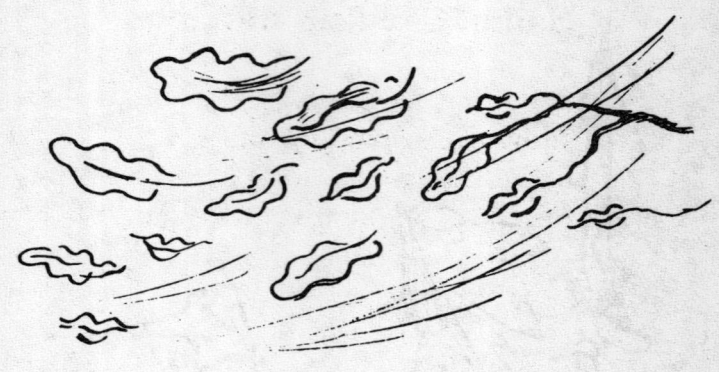

Autumn Haiku

*for the children of
Brine Leas School, Nantwich*

the high-pitched laughter
of girls outside swirls like leaves
on the Autumn wind.

Haiku: City Park in Winter

snowdrops stand up stiff
twilight nurses
round the darkening flowerbeds.

Wartime Child

1 *Tank*

Back from school along the footpath,
with the smell of elderberry-leaves and camomile,
gasmask banging against my back.
The sound of the stream under the bridge,
lost in the sudden scream of metal. Huge,
like a giant Dinky Toy, the Sherman tank
tears the tarmac as it turns. Hot breath
of engine-oil. Khaki-and-green camouflage,
a white star painted on its side.
Across the bridge, sunlight gleams
on the corner where it's chipped the stone away.
Up the path, and the smell of wallflowers.
Potato-cakes for tea today.

2 *Seaside*

The sea, and somewhere over there, the Enemy.
You can be Monty in the desert on the sandhills,
chasing the Afrika Korps. They've made more
concrete pyramids to stop them coming ashore.
Dragon's Teeth, they're called, all spaced out
as far as you can see. Poles along the beach
right out to sea. Concrete machine-gun posts
disguised as ice-cream stalls. I wonder
if they'll really come? We've all got a number

in case we get lost. ZMGM/136/3: that's me.
I've got a ration book and an identity card.
It's really hard to make sweet coupons last.
Spam and Dried Eggs for tea. When they
came back on the train some had got no clothes,
just overcoats or a blanket. They'd lost them
in the boats, I suppose. One gave me a French coin
with a hole in. Jamesie's Mum was crying.
I wonder why?

3 *Blackout*

It doesn't seem the same place after dark.
In the Park they've taken away the railings
to make guns. As soon as the sun's gone down
the whole town seems changed: it's strange,
you can't tell where the pavement is.
Auntie Margaret fell over someone's bike
the other night. Only a pale blue light
from cars. Of course, you can see the stars.
We saw one once Dad said was Mars.
When there's a moon the barrage balloons
shine like silver. So that the Germans
won't know where they are, there's no names
on the stations. We can't tell, either.
It smells of steam and soldiers sleep
on kitbags. Sometimes the Yanks give us
chewing-gum. Mum says all the shops
used to be lit up, just like you see them
in America on the cinema.
It must be nice with all the lights.

4 *Shrapnel*

This is the biggest one. It's smooth,
and comes to a point, with three ridges
round the middle. The outside edges
are jagged and starting to rust. Just
found it today. Tonight I'll put it away
in the shoe-box with the rest. The best
so far. I suppose if we'd stayed it wouldn't be
so scarce. Shrapnel everywhere. It's worse
than before, Grandad says. Grandma
hurt her arm when they were bombed out last time.
The smell of ointment when we went to see her.
I wonder if there'll be another raid tonight?
I like it in the shelter.

5 *Radio*

It was on the radio. A thousand bombers
over Cologne. I wonder what it's like up there
all alone? We're winning:
Winston told us so the other day. It's funny,
I can remember the beginning. September,
and the sun shining. Mum calling me in.
'Come quickly, listen.' Something called
an Ultimatum had expired. 'It's war,' they said.
Soon it was time for bed. I didn't feel tired.
Now we listen every night: The News,
and The Home Service. I like the funny ones best,
I.T.M.A., Much Binding and the rest.
I can do all the voices. All the places
seem so far away. Mr Jackson wrote to us
the other day. 'Somewhere in Europe' it said.
The Head pinned it up on the notice-board.
I hope he comes back.
I wonder if peace will be boring?

The Dark

I don't like the dark coming down on my head
It feels like a blanket thrown over the bed
I don't like the dark coming down on my head

I don't like the dark coming down over me
It feels like the room's full of things I can't see
I don't like the dark coming down over me

There isn't enough light from under the door
It only just reaches the edge of the floor
There isn't enough light from under the door

I wish that my dad hadn't put out the light
It feels like there's something that's just out of sight
I wish that my dad hadn't put out the light

But under the bedclothes it's warm and secure
You can't see the ceiling you can't see the floor
Yes, under the bedclothes it's warm and secure
So I think I'll stay here till it's daylight once more.

Shazia

The sun shines all the time
in Pakistan.
Here it rains and rains
except when it snows.
Even my friend Baljeet's
new pink sweater
has little black rainclouds on.
Flowers come out all the year round
in Pakistan.
Here you have to buy them from a shop
except in the summer.
All the houses are grey here
no one paints them in bright patterns
like they do
in Pakistan.
The other girls here
wear skirts that show their legs
not like my nice silk trousers.
When I go to our church
with my other friend Daljit,
I wear a red-and-gold scarf
around my head
like they do
in Pakistan.
Mum and Dad say we're better off here
than
in Pakistan.
Some of the English boys call us names.
No one calls you a Paki
in Pakistan.

Pedestrian

I've got a pain in the 96th,
or is it the 97th? I can never
remember. That side's left,
this is . . . yes, that's right,
the 96th. It's all the spiky bits
on this green thing. Oh!
now the 47th's started
to go . . . soon
I won't have one left
to stand on.

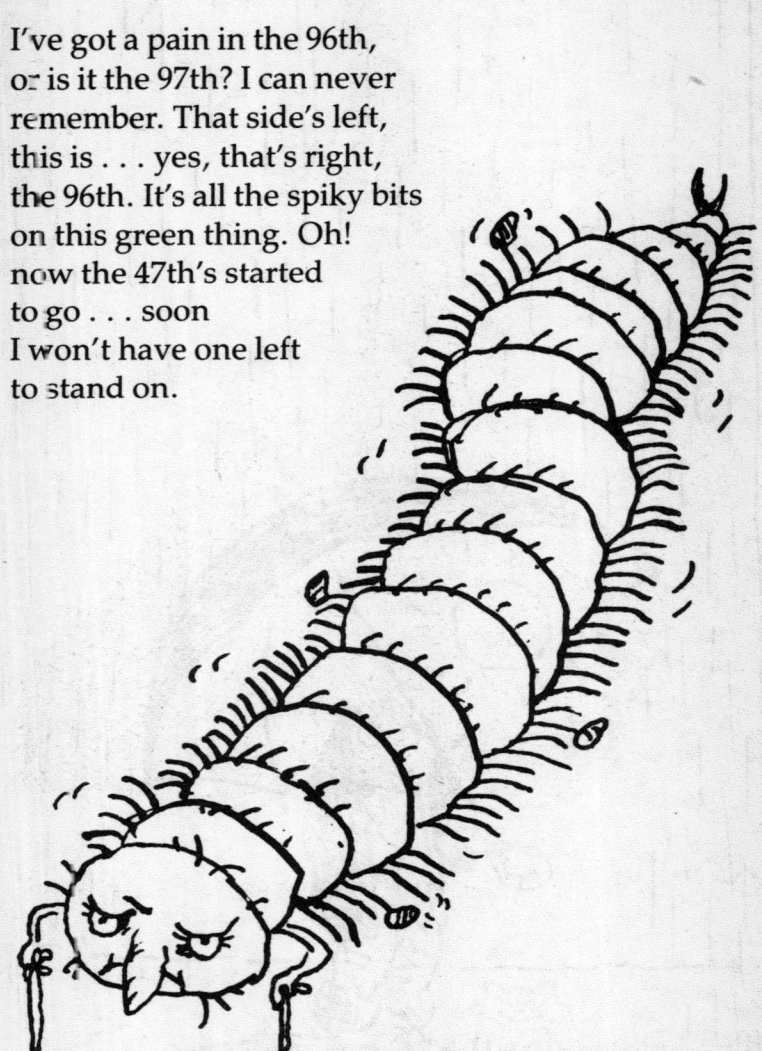

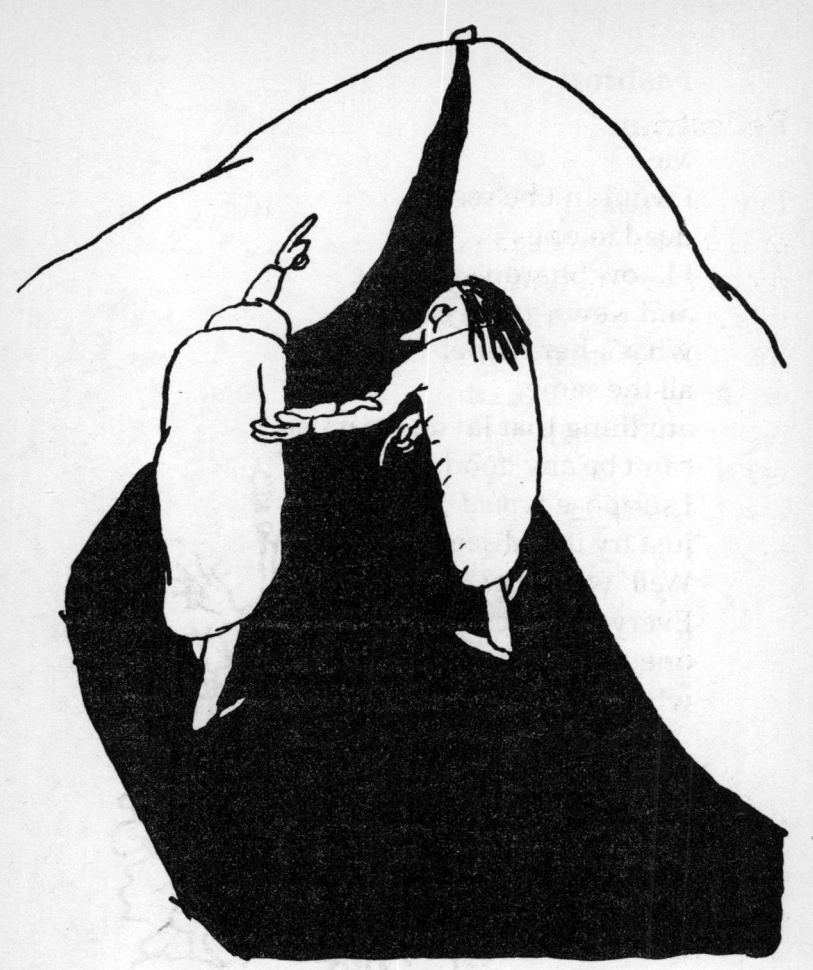

On Taking a Walk in the Pleasant Countryside

for Kit Wright

If we hadn't turned back
Before we got to the top of the hill
We wouldn't have seen the rainbow.

Fashion

Me?
I wouldn't be seen
dead in one . . .
I know Sharon's got one
and Kevin's sister
what's-her-name;
all the same,
anything that Jayne wears
can't be any good . . .
I suppose I *could*
just try it and see . . .
Well, why not?
Everyone else has got
one,
why not me?

Crowfield

They are holding
council meetings demonstrations
in the angry air
picket the October sunlight.
Flakes of burnt paper
fall towards the stubblefield.

Goalposts

'The Government's moved the goalposts'
I'm sure you've heard it before
'The Opposition have moved the goalposts'
You've read it in papers galore.
If they always know who's done it
And politicians seem terribly sure,
Why does someone invisible move them
Whenever I try to score?

The Green Light

There's a green light in at the window
There's a green light shining on the stair
There's a sound where the green light comes from
But I can't see anything there.

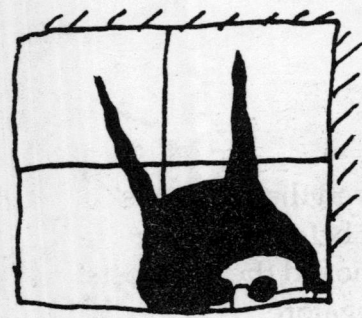

There's a green light shining from the doorway
There's a green light glows in the night
There's a shape where the green light comes from
And it's not a pretty sight.

There's a green light growing clearer
There's a green light like the sea
There's a *something* getting nearer
And I think it's after me.

There's a green light all around me
There's a green light fills the skies
There's a green light that surrounds me
And it's looking in my eyes . . .

Mr McManus

Mr McManus was a very big Mcman.
On the other hand, Mr McMahon was rather
Mcsmall, in fact not tall at all,
at all. Mr McManus was very
Mcstrong. No-one would ever say
'You're wrong, Mr McManus,' this would be
very bad manners. It would be a brave
Mcman who tried. One day Mr McMahon
forgot his Mcmanners and said 'You're wrong
Mr McManus.' Appalled at this breach
of good manners, Mr McManus held Mr McMahon
against the Mcwall. All the crowd in the Barley Mow
crowded round to see. Mr McManus was
much too Mcstrong. 'I was wrong' cried Mr McMahon
who began to quake. Mr McManus went to shake
the Mchand of Mr McMahon, who ran
for his life. Mrs McManus, McManus's wife
laughed at the sight. Now every night
there is peace in the Barley Mow (and
The Dun Cow). But Mr McMahon
was never Mcseen
again. At all,
at all.

Ideal Gnome

An old gnome sat
in an Old Gnome's Home
and talked of gardens he had known;
he sat and talked of days gone by,
of fish and frogs and dragonfly,
remembering the willowtree, the rockery
where he had stood for years and fished.
As his eyes filled with tears, he wished
that he could go back to the place
he used to know, that's now
a concrete patio. Sometimes he just sits
and dreams about the day they came
with the machines, pulled up the tree,
and poured the concrete on.
Now it's all gone.
       The Gnome's Home's
an ideal home for one old gnome
who talks of better days he's seen.
With misted eyes he sees the green weed,
watches the goldfish rise.

I'm not one. The ones they write special books for or those soppy magazines. Just because you're in your teens they think you're an idiot. Telly programmes that won't stay still for a minute, girls in tiny minis, spotty boys, wall-to-wall disco noise, tinny Walkmen walking through your head. Adverts for tampons, skin care, hair care, should you go to bed? I'm under twenty-one: does that make me a moron?

Anyway, I don't care about popularity: I'm *me*.

Teenage angst from the Liverpool poet.

Adrian Henri

PHANTOM LOLLIPOP LADY

A sparkling collection of poems especially for children by one of Britain's best-known poets.

'A new collection of poems is like a box of assorted chocolates . . . Adrian Henri's new collection is a very tasty selection. Open this tempting book yourselves and pick out your best ones . . .'
Adele Geras

'A terrific read' *Parents*

Mark Burgess

FEELING BEASTLY

I love to see the jigsaw bird
Flying upside down.
It sings a song that sounds all wrong
And wears a dressing gown.

I love to see the sawjig bird
Flying downside up.
It feeds on chips and concrete mix
And drinks them from a cup.

This anthology is bursting at the seams with
beastly poems!

William Cole and Tomi Ungerer

Selections of funny, absurd and truly ridiculous
rhymes accompanied by hilarious drawings –
guaranteed to make you giggle.

Beastly Boys and Ghastly Girls
Oh, Such Foolishness!
Oh, That's Ridiculous!
Oh, What Nonsense!

Jennifer and Graeme Curry

DOWN OUR STREET

Welcome to our street! It's a street like any other,
full of houses, shops and people – maybe it's a bit
like yours? Come and see . . .

> "It's noisy and it's dirty,
> It's crowded but it's fun . . .
> That's our street.
>
> It's waiting with a welcome,
> So follow us and come . . .
> Down our street."

An entertaining collection of original poems full
of street life.

Jennifer Curry (editor)

THE LAST RABBIT

A collection of green poems.

The natural world is beautiful. The natural world is threatened. Here are poems to celebrate the beauty and cry out against its destruction.

THE TIGER

The tiger has wise eyes.
He knows about men.
They put traps to kill him.
They will take his coat for
rich ladies to wear.
The tiger is angry.
So am I.

Vorakit Boonchareon

A Selected List of Fiction from Mammoth

While every effort is made to keep prices low, it is sometimes necessary to increase prices at short notice. Mammoth Books reserves the right to show new retail prices on covers which may differ from those previously advertised in the text or elsewhere.

The prices shown below were correct at the time of going to press.

☐	7497 0366 0	**Dilly the Dinosaur**	Tony Bradman	£1.99
☐	7497 0021 1	**Dilly and the Tiger**	Tony Bradman	£1.99
☐	7497 0137 4	**Flat Stanley**	Jeff Brown	£1.99
☐	7497 0048 3	**Friends and Brothers**	Dick King-Smith	£1.99
☐	7497 0054 8	**My Naughty Little Sister**	Dorothy Edwards	£1.99
☐	416 86550 X	**Cat Who Wanted to go Home**	Jill Tomlinson	£1.99
☐	7497 0166 8	**The Witch's Big Toe**	Ralph Wright	£1.99
☐	7497 0218 4	**Lucy Jane at the Ballet**	Susan Hampshire	£2.25
☐	416 03212 5	**I Don't Want To!**	Bel Mooney	£1.99
☐	7497 0030 0	**I Can't Find It!**	Bel Mooney	£1.99
☐	7497 0032 7	**The Bear Who Stood on His Head**	W. J. Corbett	£1.99
☐	416 10362 6	**Owl and Billy**	Martin Waddell	£1.75
☐	416 13822 5	**It's Abigail Again**	Moira Miller	£1.75
☐	7497 0031 9	**King Tubbitum and the Little Cook**	Margaret Ryan	£1.99
☐	7497 0041 6	**The Quiet Pirate**	Andrew Matthews	£1.99
☐	7497 0064 5	**Grump and the Hairy Mammoth**	Derek Sampson	£1.99

All these books are available at your bookshop or newsagent, or can be ordered direct from the publisher. Just tick the titles you want and fill in the form below.

Mandarin Paperbacks, Cash Sales Department, PO Box 11, Falmouth, Cornwall TR10 9EN.

Please send cheque or postal order, no currency, for purchase price quoted and allow the following for postage and packing:

UK — 80p for the first book, 20p for each additional book ordered to a maximum charge of £2.00.

BFPO — 80p for the first book, 20p for each additional book.

Overseas including Eire — £1.50 for the first book, £1.00 for the second and 30p for each additional book thereafter.

NAME (Block letters) ....

ADDRESS ....

....

....